75|| 1319

OBJECTIFICATION
OF WOMEN
IN THE MEDIA

BY CHRISTINE EVANS

ReferencePoint
Press®

San Diego, CA

For more information, contact:
ReferencePoint Press, Inc.
PO Box 27779
San Diego, CA 92198
www.ReferencePointPress.com

LIBRARY OF CONGRESS CATALOGING-IN-PUBLICATION DATA

Name: Evans, Christine, 1979– author.
Title: Objectification of Women in the Media/by Christine Evans.
Description: San Diego, CA: ReferencePoint Press, Inc., [2019] | Series: Women and Society
| Audience: Grade 9 to 12 | Includes bibliographical references and index.
ISBN: 978-1-68282-543-3 (hardback)
ISBN: 978-1-68282-544-0 (ebook)
The complete Library of Congress record is available at www.loc.gov.

CONTENTS

IMPORTANT EVENTS IN
WOMEN'S HISTORY

1985
The Bechdel test is created by cartoonist Alison Bechdel to critically analyze the role of women in movies.

1941
The first television ad airs in the United States, providing a new platform for advertising media.

1972
Gloria Steinem and Dorothy Pitman Hughes launch *Ms.* magazine, a feminist publication.

1848
Women start the women's suffrage movement to fight for their right to vote.

| 1850 | 1900 | 1950 | 1975 | 2000 |

1883
One of the first magazines for women, *Ladies' Home Journal*, launches.

1979
Jean Kilbourne releases her first *Killing Us Softly* documentary discussing the objectification of women in advertising.

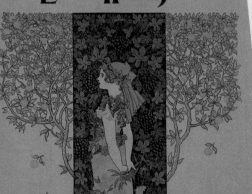

THE LADIES' HOME JOURNAL

1965
Prominent women's magazine *Cosmopolitan* shifts its focus to young women with content about sex, birth control, and business careers.

1996
The first *Tomb Raider* video game is released, featuring a female hero, Lara Croft.

2004
Dove, a cosmetics company, launches its Real Beauty campaign to focus on a message of positive, realistic body images for women.

2011
The *Miss Representation* documentary is released, highlighting the objectification of women in media.

2017
The first Women's March protest is attended by approximately 4 million people globally.

2000 **2005** **2010** **2015** **2020**

2003
Media mogul Oprah Winfrey becomes the first black woman to be recognized on *Forbes* magazine's list of billionaires.

2014
Online clothing store ModCloth publicly pledges to stop altering photographs of models.

2016
Truth in Advertising legislation is proposed in the United States to regulate digital alteration of photographs used in advertising.

2005
The Women's Media Center is formed by Jane Fonda, Robin Morgan, and Gloria Steinem.

2018
CVS Pharmacy pledges to stop airbrushing photographs in beauty advertisements.

WHAT IS OBJECTIFICATION?

A young woman leans back on a bed with her legs open alongside the slogan "Now Open."[1] What is she advertising? American Apparel clothing. Another woman, apparently dead, is in a car trunk while a man poses with a shovel. They're advertising Jimmy Choo shoes. A giant billboard showcases a woman in a bikini and asks, "Are you Beach Body Ready?"[2] The sign advertises weight-loss products. In all of these advertisements, the women are treated as objects. Objectification is when a person, often a woman, is viewed as an object. The focus is often only on her body. Her personality, skills, and accomplishments are ignored. This objectification of women is widespread in media today, from advertisements and magazines to movies and TV shows.

"Everyday, ordinary women are being reduced to their sexual body parts," says Sarah Gervais, a psychologist at the University of Nebraska, Lincoln.[3]

> "Everyday, ordinary women are being reduced to their sexual body parts."[3]
> – *Sarah Gervais, psychologist*

Women are often portrayed as sex objects in advertising and entertainment media. This objectification can negatively affect how people view all women.

Her research shows that people's brains process images of men as whole beings but women as a collection of objects. Gervais added that the media is a prime suspect for causing people to view women's bodies as parts: "Women's bodies and their body parts are used to sell all sorts of products, but we are now for everyday, ordinary women, processing them in a similar way."[4] Sexually objectified women are no longer seen as human—instead, they're seen as less competent and less worthy of empathy by both men and women. One study even revealed that people are less concerned about a person's pain when the person is presented as a sex object.

SELF-OBJECTIFICATION

This objectification by society and the media can lead to self-objectification, which means women and girls can start to view themselves as objects, too. For example, appearance may become overly important, and a woman may spend more time thinking about, and criticizing, her own appearance. "Not only are girls seen as objects by other people, they learn to see themselves as objects," activist Jean Kilbourne said in the 2011 documentary *Miss Representation*.[5] The more that women and girls carry out this self-objectification, the more likely they are to be depressed, suffer from eating disorders, have low confidence and ambition, and score lower on school tests. According to *Miss Representation*, 53 percent of thirteen-year-old girls are unhappy with their bodies. This number increases to 78 percent by the time they reach age seventeen.

> "Not only are girls seen as objects by other people, they learn to see themselves as objects."[5]
> – Jean Kilbourne, activist

MEDIA AND OBJECTIFICATION

Research has shown that self-objectification can stem directly from images in the media. The American Psychological Association reported that images in media and advertising encourage girls to focus on looks and sexuality in ways that are harmful to their emotional and physical health. Media objectification can leave girls and women feeling like they are expected to conform to the media's ideals just so they can fit in and be attractive. It can seem to women that their accomplishments don't matter as much as what they look like, what they wear, and how much they weigh. Body image issues can start as early as kindergarten. A study by Common Sense Media, an organization that educates children and their parents about media, concluded that girls as young as age six were dissatisfied with their bodies.

When the media objectifies women, it can leave girls and women feeling self-conscious about their own bodies. Girls and women often start to objectify themselves after seeing women objectified in media.

In the 2016 documentary *Embrace*, Taryn Brumfitt interviewed women and asked them to describe their bodies. The responses included: "Not perfect," "Wobbly," "Not nice to look at," and "I hate it. I feel disgusting."[6] According to *Embrace*, of all the cosmetic procedures performed in the world, 86.3 percent were on women. In the United States alone, there were 17.5 million cosmetic procedures performed in 2017, a 2 percent increase compared with 2016. Procedures included breast augmentation, nose reshaping, liposuction, and facelifts, as well as less-invasive treatments like botox, chemical peels, and laser hair removal. According to the American Academy of Facial Plastic and Reconstructive Surgery (AAFPRS), 13 percent of facial plastic surgeons surveyed in 2014 reported seeing more patients requesting surgeries to make them resemble celebrities such as Angelina Jolie and Beyoncé. A 2013 British study showed that women expressed an increased desire to have cosmetic surgery when they were exposed to certain words—such as *sexiness*, *physique*, and *beauty*—that could trigger self-objectification. The researchers concluded that printed words (such as words in a magazine) that contain sexually objectifying content are enough to increase women's self-objectification and body shame, making them more likely to want cosmetic surgery.

The objectification of women in media doesn't just affect women and girls. Young men and boys who see the perfect, digitally enhanced photos of supermodels and actors then expect unattainable standards of beauty from girls and women in real life. Plus, research suggests that the objectification of women can lead to increased violence against women.

> "Turning a human being into a thing is almost always the first step toward justifying violence against that person."[7]
> – Jean Kilbourne, activist

"Turning a human being into a thing is almost always the first step toward justifying violence against that person," Kilbourne said in *Miss Representation*.[7] The international nonprofit organization UNICEF reports that approximately 60,000 adolescent girls die each year as a result of violence. Across the world, 120 million girls have been victims of forced sexual acts including rape. And an estimated 11 percent of high school girls in the United States report that they have been raped. UNICEF says, "When women and girls are repeatedly objectified and their bodies hypersexualized, the media contributes to harmful gender stereotypes that often trivialize violence against girls."[8]

Regardless of women's accomplishments, the message that it matters how girls and women look is frequently repeated in media such as movies, sports programming, TV shows, advertising, and magazines. Media shapes everything—politics, policy, and how people feel about themselves and their world. So, understanding the history of objectification and how media affects women in the twenty-first century is an important step in overcoming stereotypes and gender imbalance.

"When women and girls are repeatedly objectified and their bodies hypersexualized, the media contributes to harmful gender stereotypes that often trivialize violence against girls."[8]
— UNICEF, an international nonprofit organization

CHAPTER ONE

HAVE WOMEN ALWAYS BEEN OBJECTIFIED?

||||

Elizabeth Cady Stanton, a famous American suffragist who pursued women's right to vote, said in 1880, "I would have girls regard themselves not as adjectives but nouns, not mere appendages made to qualify somebody else."[9] At the time of Stanton's speech, women weren't allowed to vote, married women couldn't own their own houses, and women couldn't even wear pants. The world was a place where men were in charge, and women were seen as being owned by men—first by their fathers and later by their husbands. Historically, women and girls were considered things to be owned, essentially objects. And the media of the time perpetuated that view.

PRINT MEDIA

Magazines for women started appearing in the nineteenth century, including *Ladies' Home Journal* and *Godey's Lady's Book*. These magazines began to introduce lifestyle advice and recipes with the goal of appealing to women who were managing their families and households. Fashion started making an appearance, too. Companies soon realized

Ladies' Home Journal was first published in 1883. It was one of the first women's magazines and was still being published in 2018.

that these magazines were an opportunity to advertise products to women. Thanks to advertising revenues, the publisher of *Ladies' Home Journal* could keep prices low, and the magazine increased its circulation to 1 million monthly subscribers in 1903.

Advertising agencies started to form, and ads not only filled magazines and newspapers but also adorned billboards and streetcars. In the 1930s, during the Great Depression, ads showing beautiful women carrying out domestic tasks started appearing in order to sell products. "Women dressed in heels and pearls were shown scrubbing a floor, or baking a pie," wrote Jennifer Nelson in *Airbrushed Nation*.[10] The narrative shifted during World War II (1939–1945) when women were encouraged by advertising to contribute to the war effort by filling the jobs left behind by the men who went to fight overseas. But by the 1950s, magazines were once again talking about a woman's place in home and family life. A 1952 advertisement for coffee showed a woman being hit by her husband for not buying the freshest coffee in the store. This ad, which was supposed to be humorous, reflected the attitudes of the time—domestic abuse was seen as something to tell a joke about to sell coffee. According to advertisers of the 1950s, a woman's purpose was to keep her husband happy.

But some women were rejecting the way they were being portrayed. Julia Ashenhurst, a housewife, was given a makeover in *Ladies' Home Journal.* Her waist was cinched in with a corset, her hair was changed, and she was dressed in new clothes. Ashenhurst complained that magazines portrayed an ideal that women could not live up to: "How will my counterpart in apartments, farms, and developments all over the country feel as she sees this glamorous clotheshorse and realizes she can't afford to dress like that and wonders why she cannot look like that?"[11]

THE INFLUENCE OF TELEVISION

Television opened up a whole new avenue for advertisers. The first TV commercial, which advertised a watch, appeared in July 1941. Early television commercials targeting women included ads for cigarettes, hair color, and soap. By 1951, there were 12 million televisions in the United States beaming the news and other programs into homes. By the 1960s, ABC, CBS, NBC, and PBS were broadcasting a variety of shows, from *The Mickey Mouse Club* to *I Love Lucy.* Women were featured in some TV roles during this era. *I Love Lucy*'s protagonist was a housewife who longed for a life in show business, but her husband believed a woman's

WHAT WOMEN

(cover text:)
COSMOPOLITAN

What Men Crave in July

HIS 6 SECRET SEX SPOTS
Master Your Guy's Biggest Below-the-Belt Pleasure Triggers

50 Things You Should Have Never Stopped Doing

Rihanna
She Finally Reveals Her Deepest Feelings

YOUR BREAST MYTHS— BUSTED
#1: The Boobgasm Does Exist

Talking Tricks That Draw Him In
p. 98

APRIL 2014

Little Liars' Ashley son
ebCrush

'RE LE Y?
NS EN IE, ID

Cosmopolitan introduced a new type of women's magazine in the 1960s, focused on sex, birth control, and other topics geared toward single women. The magazine was still popular in 2018.

place was in the home. Another popular show was *I Dream of Jeannie*, a sitcom about a 2,000-year-old genie sprung from her bottle by her so-called "master," a male astronaut who falls in love with her.

The rise of television meant that magazines had to change their appeal. Publishers started targeting audiences with niche magazines such as home and decorating magazines, fashion magazines, and fitness magazines. By the 1960s, editors at *Cosmopolitan* magazine recognized that single women with a disposable income were interested in reading about issues such as sex and birth control. New magazines opened up more opportunities for brands looking to market their products to women.

The 1970s were a time of change for women—but there was a gap between what happened in real life and what happened in TV commercials. Women no longer accepted that they had to get married, start a family, and become dedicated homemakers. But advertisements still showed women in those roles. One of the earliest protests against advertising occurred in 1969 when protesters objected to the portrayal of girls in a *Life* magazine ad. The ad for Mattel toys showed girls dreaming of becoming ballerinas as boys were portrayed as being born to build and invent. In 1971, National Airlines raised an outcry when it ran ads with images of women along with the tagline, "I'm Cheryl. Fly me."[12] The ads also said, "I'm a girl. I'm an airplane. I'm a fresh way to get you where you want to go!"[13] While the campaign was running, stewardesses for the airline had to wear a button with the slogan "Fly Me."[14] Writer and activist Gloria Steinem said, "Advertising is a very important form of education. It is estimated that 40 percent of all our subcultural intake comes from advertising."[15] So when advertising is portraying women as objects, that becomes part of the surrounding culture. The advertising industry did partly seem to take notice. Some advertisements changed and reflected the messages that feminists were concerned with: Don't treat women as sex objects, weak, or inferior; don't limit women to being wives and mothers; and don't put limitations on young girls. In 1973, Revlon's advertisement for Charlie perfume showed a confident young woman in a pantsuit striding through London. Clairol, a company that sells hair products, soon depicted mothers as jockeys, filmmakers, doctors, politicians, and artists.

MS. MAGAZINE

In 1972, Steinem and fellow activist Dorothy Pitman Hughes launched a new magazine. Titled *Ms.*, it had glossy pages, advertisements, and how-to articles like any other popular women's magazine. But the cover featured empowering images including the female superhero Wonder Woman, and the how-to section included articles on how to win a

**Gloria Steinem has remained a prominent feminist activist since she cofounded
Ms. magazine in 1972. She speaks at many events and rallies in support
of equality.**

promotion or how to run a public protest. The magazine was run by
women, for women, and the advertisements reflected that. Women, the
editors said, do not spend half their income on lipsticks and perfumes—
they also buy stereos, televisions, cars, and tools. So those were the kinds
of products that were advertised in *Ms.* It seemed a change had come to
advertising and media.

However, a lot of media still stereotype and objectify women. In
a review of 1,000 *Rolling Stone* cover images published over four
decades, researchers found that sexualized representations of both

men and women have become more common over time. In the 1960s, 11 percent of men and 44 percent of women on the *Rolling Stone* covers were considered sexualized. In the 2000s, 17 percent of men and 83 percent of women were sexualized in cover photos. Sociologist Erin Hatton concluded, "Popular media outlets such as *Rolling Stone* are not depicting women as sexy musicians or actors; they are depicting women musicians and actors as ready and available for sex."[16] In other words, instead of having their professional success highlighted as an attractive feature, the focus was on these actors' and musicians' bodies.

> "Popular media outlets such as *Rolling Stone* are not depicting women as sexy musicians or actors; they are depicting women musicians and actors as ready and available for sex."[16]
> – Erin Hatton, sociologist

MOVIE STARS TO SEX OBJECTS

Women have not only been objectified in print media and on TV. Movie stars have long been subjected to the same scrutiny. Marilyn Monroe hit the screens in the 1950s. In 1955, a *New York Times* headline screamed, "LOOK AT MARILYN!"[17] The article went on to describe her as portraying a "sexy empty-headed dame" in *The Seven Year Itch*.[18] Hugh Hefner published Monroe's nude photograph in the first edition of his *Playboy* magazine—even though she never signed an agreement to be featured. Monroe herself said in 1962, "I never quite understood it, this sex symbol. I always thought symbols were those things you clash together! That's the trouble, a sex symbol becomes a thing. I just hate to be a thing."[19] Monroe was one of the early female celebrities to be objectified by the media. But she certainly wasn't the last.

> "I never quite understood it, this sex symbol. I always thought symbols were those things you clash together! That's the trouble, a sex symbol becomes a thing. I just hate to be a thing."[19]
> – actress Marilyn Monroe in 1962

The *James Bond* films always feature the British male spy saving the day. The first *Bond* film, *Dr. No*, was released in 1962 and starred Sean Connery. Ursula Andress played the first so-called Bond Girl. When she first appears in the film, she is emerging from the ocean in a white bikini while being watched by a hidden Bond. "What are you doing here? Looking for shells?" she asks. He replies, "No, I'm just looking."[20] Such scenes in the *Bond* films are an example of the male gaze. Laura Mulvey, a British feminist who studies films, described the male gaze as when a movie (or other media) is "constructed for the pleasure of the male viewer."[21] This means that male viewers are the target audience, and therefore their needs are met first. Mulvey said that this problem stems from an old-fashioned, male-driven society. When movies are made from the perspective of men, audiences have no choice but to view women from the point-of-view of a heterosexual man—no matter what their own gender or sexual orientation is. Close-up shots of women from over a man's shoulder, shots that linger on a woman's body, or scenes in which a man watches a passive woman are all indications that the movie has been produced from the perspective of a man. Examples of the male gaze and media objectification of women on screen are repeated again and again throughout film history.

THE IMPACT OF MEDIA OBJECTIFICATION

Media influences people's behavior. A 2015 study by Common Sense Media said that teenagers spend approximately nine hours a day engaging with some type of media, including TV shows, movies, music, video games, and social media. Those nine hours don't include using media at school or for homework. The study discovered a difference between girls and boys: Girls spent more time on social media than boys did, while boys spent more time on video games. James Steyer, chief executive officer and founder of Common Sense Media, said, "It just shows you that these kids live in this massive 24/7 digital media

WHEN TV ARRIVED IN FIJI

In the Pacific island nation of Fiji, prosperity has traditionally been associated with food and therefore with a fuller figure. But after television arrived on the island in 1995, Fiji was struck by an outbreak of eating disorders. Harvard researchers said, "The western images and values transmitted via the medium has led to an increase in disorders such as anorexia and bulimia."[1] Thirty-eight months after the first TV station on the island went on air, 74 percent of teenage girls surveyed felt they were "too big or fat."[2] According to anthropologist Anne Becker, nobody was dieting in Fiji before television arrived, but "an alarmingly high percentage of adolescents are dieting now." One young Fijian woman told Becker, "The actresses and all those girls, especially those European girls, I just like, I just admire them and want to be like them. I want their body, I want their size. I want myself to be in the same position as they are."[3]

1. Quoted in "TV Brings Eating Disorders to Fiji," BBC News, May 20, 1999. news.bbc.co.uk.
2. Quoted in "TV Brings Eating Disorders to Fiji."
3. Anne E. Becker, "Television, Disordered Eating, and Young Women in Fiji: Negotiating Body Image and Identity during Rapid Social Change," Culture, Medicine and Psychiatry, December 2004, p. 546.

technology world, and it's shaping every aspect of their life. They spend far more time with media technology than any other thing in their life."[22] A 2017 study discovered that just thirty minutes of Instagram use can lead to an increase of self-objectification.

The advertising industry is worth more than $200 billion in the United States, and, according to Jean Kilbourne in her documentary *Killing Us Softly*, the average American is exposed to more than 3,000 brand messages a day. Ads are everywhere, from bus stops to schools to billboards to airplanes. Every aspect of people's lives is invaded by media and advertising. Advertising is even happening during movies when a product is mentioned. For example, a movie's main character might pour soda from a bottle with the brand purposefully shown on screen. Ads are often selling ideas, including ideas about what the ideal woman should look like. They encourage people to buy products to achieve that ideal. Over time, exposure to constant media messages about what a woman's role should be can leave women feeling disempowered.

This feeling of disempowerment may make women less likely to pursue leadership roles in careers such as politics, an area in which women are underrepresented.

For example, during both her bid for the 2008 Democratic presidential nomination, as well as during her 2016 presidential campaign, Hillary Clinton was subjected to media headlines such as, "Here's What Hillary Looks Like After Paying $600 for a Haircut that Shut Down an Entire Salon."[23] Another headline read, "Hillary Clinton's Tentative Dip into New Neckline Territory."[24] It could be argued that male politicians are sometimes similarly objectified. For example, one headline about Canadian Prime Minister Justin Trudeau asked, "Is Justin Trudeau the sexiest politician in the world?"[25] Another headline said, "Canada's hot new prime minister has the Internet sweating maple syrup."[26] But the difference is that men are already in positions of power; they're already in the highest political offices and business leadership positions. As Georgina Dent wrote in the magazine *Marie Claire*, "Like most men, Trudeau's worth might be boosted, in the eyes of some, by virtue of his good looks, but his looks aren't definitive. His worth, his power, and his authority are all far bigger than his appearance."[27] In contrast, most female leaders are constantly compared and scrutinized for their looks as they work to rise up to positions of power.

Objectification doesn't just affect women hoping to lead the country. To prove that the media affects how everyday people feel about themselves, researchers investigated the role of visual media by looking at the relationship between body image issues and abnormal eating attitudes in visually impaired women. They recruited sixty women—twenty were blind from birth, twenty were blinded in later life, and twenty were not blind. The researchers asked each woman about her body shape and her attitudes toward eating. The women who had always been blind and therefore had never seen any visual media that objectified women had significantly lower body dissatisfaction scores and more positive eating

HOW TO IDENTIFY OBJECTIFYING IMAGES

Caroline Heldman, a politics professor at Occidental College in Los Angeles, California, described seven categories of images that show people as objects. If an image falls into one or more of these categories, it's considered an objectifying image:

1. Does the image show only part of a person's body?
2. Does the image show a person standing in for an object? For example, a woman's legs become the legs of a table.
3. Does the image show the person as being interchangeable with others? For example, an ad may show several women who look identical.
4. Does the image affirm the idea of violating a person who can't consent?
5. Does the image suggest that the defining characteristic of the person is his or her sexual availability?
6. Does the image show a person's body as a commodity that can be bought or sold? For example, an ad for shoes showed women available for purchase from a vending machine.
7. Does the image use the person's body as a canvas? For example, an advertising slogan might be written on a woman's body.

attitudes compared with women who were blinded later in life and sighted women. Studies like this one suggest that visual media messages are leading to increasing numbers of women and girls being dissatisfied with their bodies.

WHO IS BEHIND THE MEDIA?

So, who is making the decisions that lead to objectification of women in media? It's mostly men. Women are underrepresented in most media organizations. According to the Women's Media Center (WMC), "Women are not equal partners in telling the story, nor are they equal partners in sourcing and interpreting what and who is important in the story."[28] For example, men reported three times more news than women did in 2017 on the major TV networks ABC, CBS, and NBC. As Steinem, who cofounded the WMC, said in a press release, "When men or women turn to or on the media, yet fail to see women in our true diversity, there is a sense that all or some women literally don't count. It's crucial that the media report and reflect, not conceal and distort."[29] In print, men report

61.9 percent of the news, while women report 38.1 percent.

For women of color, the statistics get bleaker. In 2018, the WMC reported that in the United States, women of color make up just 7.95 percent of print newsroom staff members, 12.6 percent of local TV news staff members, and 6.2 percent of local radio staff members. "Women are more than half the U.S. population, and people of color nearly 40 percent," said Julie Burton, president of the WMC. "But you wouldn't know this from our media—because U.S. media does not look like, sound like, or reflect the diversity and experience of more than half the population."[30]

It's a problem when people can't see themselves represented in the media around them. People can relate to and aspire to the people they see in media. If girls and women don't see many women represented in media, then they don't have those options for relatable role models. For that reason, the Geena Davis Institute on Gender in Media has this slogan: "If she can see it, she can be it."[31] Research from the institute shows that in film and TV, women make up only 7 percent of directors, 13 percent of writers, and 20 percent of producers. If the people behind the camera aren't representative of the population, it's likely that the characters being portrayed on screen won't be either. In fact, the institute reports that even G-rated family films fail to represent the population accurately—there are three times more boy characters than girls. Until the people behind the media change, can the movies, television shows, advertisements, and video games that people are exposed to every day change?

CHAPTER TWO

HOW ARE WOMEN OBJECTIFIED IN ADVERTISING?

Brands spend a total of $600 billion a year, globally, on advertisements. This means advertisements are everywhere, whether it's before a YouTube video, on Instagram, or in a magazine. Advertising doesn't just sell products; it sells aspirations and identities. Advertising often intentionally makes people feel anxious and insecure so that these people will then buy the advertised products to feel better and to look more like the images portrayed in the ads. For example, advertisements for face washes make people feel unhappy about their skin so they will go buy the face wash. Ads for anti-aging serums leave women thinking they need the latest technology to reduce their wrinkles. A clothing company that puts out an advertisement showing happy young people wearing its clothes is selling that young, happy lifestyle. And with the internet more available than ever before, including to children, ads directed toward adults are also being seen by kids. It is almost impossible for companies to guarantee that their advertising messages are only being seen by the age group for which they are intended.

People see dozens of advertisements every day, from billboards to catalogs to TV commercials. Many of the images in these advertisements hypersexualize and objectify women.

THE PORTRAYAL OF WOMEN IN ADVERTISING

According to a study commissioned by the cosmetics company Dove, by the time they reach age twelve, girls have seen 77,500 advertisements. For the study, girls kept diaries of the beauty images they were exposed to during daily life over three days. They wrote down their reactions to the advertisements. One fourteen-year-old girl wrote: "The images I see in magazines make me feel sad because I know I could never be that beautiful."[32] Susie Orbach, a psychotherapist and author, said, "Young girls are bombarded by millions of images of digitally manipulated, airbrushed beauty every day, and research tells us this onslaught can often be responsible for feelings of low self-esteem."[33]

> "Young girls are bombarded by millions of images of digitally manipulated, airbrushed beauty every day, and research tells us this onslaught can often be responsible for feelings of low self-esteem."[33]
> – Susie Orbach, psychotherapist and author

A 2017 study by the Geena Davis Institute on Gender in Media found that TV and film advertisements featured twice as many male characters as female characters. A quarter of the ads featured just men, compared with 5 percent that had only women. In the advertisements studied, one out of ten female characters was dressed in sexually revealing clothing—six times more than the number of men dressed in a similar way. Plus, men were 62 percent more likely to be portrayed as someone who had a career such as doctor or scientist. In fact, one-third of men were shown to have a job, while only one-quarter of women were. And when the researchers examined the settings of the advertisements, they found that women were more likely to be shown in the kitchen. It's the twenty-first century, yet many ads featuring women are still full of 1950s-era stereotypes. "By changing the narrative, the images we use, the stories we tell about women, we can dramatically change the way the world values women and how women and girls see themselves," said Madeline Di Nonno, CEO of the Geena Davis Institute. "It's not enough to portray more women. We need a more progressive and inclusive representation of women."[34] Men are present on screen more than women across all ad categories. The number of female characters, their time on screen, and their speaking time have not improved in more than a decade. Caroline Heldman, research advisor to the Geena Davis Institute, said, "We have to write female characters with more screen time, more speaking time, more prominence in the storyline, with more personal agency, and without objectifying them."[35] Eighty-five percent of women say they are offended by stereotypical depictions of their gender.

In many advertisements, women are diminished to just parts of their bodies. For example, women's breasts are used to sell everything from fishing line to cars. Even when selling products made for women, such as bras, women's breasts are used in a way to suggest that the reason to buy the product is to please men. For example, in 1994, Wonderbra used the slogan "Hello Boys" to advertise its bras.[36]

"By changing the narrative, the images we use, the stories we tell about women, we can dramatically change the way the world values women and how women and girls see themselves. It's not enough to portray more women. We need a more progressive and inclusive representation of women."[34]
– Madeline Di Nonno, CEO of the Geena Davis Institute on Gender in Media

Sexualized images have always been featured in advertising, but there has been an increase in both the volume of these images and the extent to which they are intruding on everyday life, wrote Linda Papadopoulos, who has researched how the sexualization of young girls relates to violence against women. "How have sex, sexiness and sexualisation gained such favour in recent years as to be the measure by which women's and girls' worth is judged? While it is not a new phenomenon by any means, there is something different about the way it occurs today and how it impacts on younger and younger girls," Papadopoulos said.[37] Children are being portrayed in mature ways while adult women are infantilized. Girls are sent the message that they should do whatever it takes to be desired, and boys are taught to relate to girls as sexual objects. Researchers have found that young teens post sexually explicit images of themselves on social networking sites, a pattern that is potentially a result of the normalization of sexual images through advertising and other mass media.

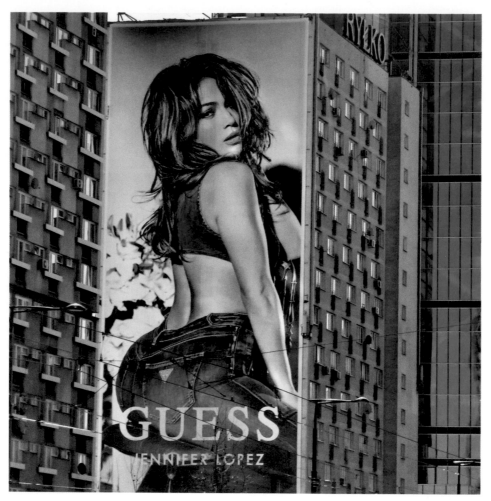

Women are objectified in advertisements selling all types of products, including clothing, cars, food, and more. This billboard selling blue jeans features actress and singer Jennifer Lopez.

WOMEN IN PRINT ADVERTISEMENTS

One segment of advertising that sexualizes women and girls is print advertising. Print advertising includes the images that appear in magazines, in catalogs, and on billboards. Advertisements that present images of young, thin, beautiful women lead to ideals of perfection that are difficult to reach—even the real-life models don't look like their photos. This is in part thanks to the advertising industry's practice of airbrushing photographs. Airbrushing means digitally altering a photograph to conceal flaws or add details that weren't there when the photograph was taken. These airbrushed images encourage people to believe in an ideal that does not exist. Research shows that these images can be particularly harmful to people between ages ten and nineteen.

Adobe Photoshop, a software program used to digitally alter images, was invented in 1987. But even before Photoshop and digital photography were widely used, photo editors could manipulate photographs in magazines. It would take hours of painstaking work by hand using film in a darkroom, but editors could over- or under-expose images to remove perceived flaws, such as fine lines, among other photo development tricks.

A famous early example of altering images in media was in 1989 when *TV Guide* magazine spliced an image of TV host and actor Oprah Winfrey's head onto an image of the body of another woman. The resulting image showed Winfrey in a revealing sparkly dress sitting on a pile of money, with a body that wasn't hers. The body belonged to actor Ann-Margret, who said at the time, "I've been on the cover of *TV Guide* four times, but never without my head."[38] Winfrey's spokesperson said in the *New York Times* that Winfrey "would never have agreed to pose in such a revealing dress, or on a pile of cash."[39] More recently, in 2018, Winfrey was pictured on the magazine *Vanity Fair's* website. Due to a poor Photoshop job, the image showed Winfrey with three hands. Winfrey responded by joking about her "third hand" on Twitter, and the magazine apologized.[40]

Today, anyone with a smartphone can alter a photo before posting it on social media. In 2014, Melissa Wells, an Instagram and Samsung smartphone user, posted about the phone automatically applying a beauty filter on her selfie: "Thanks @samsungmobile for the vote of confidence, I think I'll keep my freckles and imperfections since this is how I look in 3D and this is how all my friends see me in real life."[41]

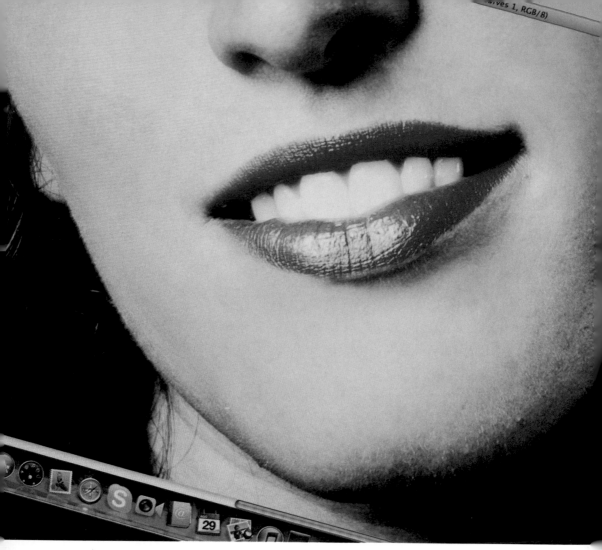

Advertisers often alter photos of models using Adobe Photoshop or other photo-editing programs. This can result in ads that feature women looking unrealistically flawless.

This easy access to airbrushing technology means it's rare to see a photograph in the media that hasn't been digitally altered in some way. Dove conducted a study of more than 1,000 women in 2009. More than two-thirds of the women stated that they lacked confidence about their bodies after seeing digitally altered images of models. Plus, one-quarter said that images in ads made them feel self-conscious. Nearly all the women said they wanted advertisers to be honest about how much they had altered the images in the ads. In 2018, Dove announced plans to start labeling its ads with a "No Digital Distortion Mark" by January 2019 so consumers can identify which ads include images that have been altered.[42]

Some models have spoken out against digital alteration of images. Model Julia Geier said, "We've spent the last five years perfecting our bodies and our skin and our hair color, and we have a team of makeup artists, and we have a team of hairstylists, and we have a team of wardrobe stylists. Then we have a professional photographer. And then all the photos get edited and Photoshopped. So the end result is the farthest thing from like a realistic photo that you can ever imagine. Women are seeing these images that literally are not real."[43]

Children in particular are not able to critically evaluate media and understand they're not viewing reality, so they're more easily influenced by what they see in advertisements. This means children are more likely to internalize the messages they see about how women and girls should look and behave, and they are more likely to think that that is what they should do and look like, too. This can lead to unhealthy behaviors, such as sexual activity at a young age or excessive dieting, as girls try to be more like the images they see in media.

HOW TV COMMERCIALS OBJECTIFY WOMEN

Women are not only objectified in print photographs. They're also sexualized and idealized in TV commercials. For example, Super Bowl commercial spots are the most sought-after in TV advertising, with a 30-second commercial selling for $5 million. But those commercials often objectify women. In an objectifying 2003 commercial, two women enjoy lunch with a light beer—but a fight soon breaks out over whether it's a good beer because of its "great taste" or because it's "less filling."[44] The women end up pulling off each other's clothes and rolling around in a fountain and in freshly poured concrete with the commercial showing

Children are particularly susceptible to the images shown in media. When children see objectifying images of women in advertising, they can internalize the message that women are objects.

plenty of close-up views of their breasts. A 2003 study looked at seventy-two randomly selected beer and non-beer ads. The researchers discovered that 75 percent of the beer ads and 50 percent of non-beer ads were considered sexist and objectified women. In a 2015 Super Bowl commercial, model Charlotte McKinney advertised burgers for Carl's Jr. Her full body is not shown right away, and the commercial suggests she

BRAND MASCOTS

The Geena Davis Institute on Gender in Media investigated gender representation in brand mascots. A mascot is a cartoon or other character used in advertisements and other materials to sell products. "We felt it was important to examine mascots for consumer goods because that area had never been extensively researched before, and mascots are a significant influence in kids' lives, similar to popular characters in TV and film," said Geena Davis, actor and activist. The institute looked at how women and people of color are represented among the mascots of the top-selling products in the United States. The study showed that male mascots outnumbered female mascots two to one. One in four of the female mascots were presented as gender stereotypes, such as being in a kitchen. Conversely, men were shown playing sports. And the mascots also represented racial stereotypes—for example, mascots depicting people of color were twice as likely to be portrayed as threatening than mascots showing white people. Exposure to mascots based on racial stereotypes or sexually objectified women increases bias against these groups.

Quoted in "Male Brand Mascots Outnumber Female Mascots Two-To-One from First Systematic Study of Mascot Gender and Race Representations Conducted by the Geena Davis Institute on Gender in Media for The Jel Sert Company," Geena Davis Institute on Gender in Media, May 9, 2018. www.seejane.org.

is naked as she walks down a busy street while men stop and stare. At one point, two melons stand in for her breasts, and a tomato is shown to represent her bottom. The ad eventually shows that she's wearing a bikini top and shorts, and she enthusiastically eats a Carl's Jr. burger at the end of the commercial.

These advertisements are clearly aimed at heterosexual men. But according to data from 2011 to 2015, women made up nearly one-half of the Super Bowl audience, and women are estimated to make 85 percent of all consumer purchases, from cars to computers to food. The commercials from more recent Super Bowls suggest that the objectification and sexualization of women is decreasing. However, women still aren't equally represented in the advertisements. In 2017, men were featured in lead roles in Super Bowl advertisements 2.5 times as often as women. Mina Enayati-Uzeta, a thirteen-year-old writer, watched the 2018 Super Bowl commercials. Enayati-Uzeta applauded Coca-Cola, which "not only showed more women than any of [the] other ads put together but also made a point of recognizing non-binary pronouns [personal pronouns other than *him* or *her*]."[45] However, several other companies disappointed Enayati-Uzeta with the lack of equal representation in their commercials. For example, the Pringles chips commercial featured three white men. Enayati-Uzeta explained why she believes representation matters: "It's really no fun if you're watching commercial after commercial featuring people who look or feel nothing like you."[46]

> "It's really no fun if you're watching commercial after commercial featuring people who look or feel nothing like you."[46]
>
> – Mina Enayati-Uzeta, writer

While it seems Super Bowl advertising may have started to change, there are still many examples of commercials that objectify and sexualize women, using them as props to sell their products. In a 2017 commercial for a new alcoholic beverage, Santo Mezquila, a woman climbs into an empty bathtub wearing lingerie and high heels to sip her drink and suggestively suck on an ice cube. About Face, a nonprofit that teaches girls how to critically assess media, reacted negatively to the commercial by saying, "Really, what the heck!? This is about as explicit as sexist media gets!"[47]

INTERNET AND SOCIAL MEDIA

While traditional television viewing is decreasing and print magazine sales flounder, the internet is everywhere. Many children and teenagers have easy access to smartphones, tablets, and computers. Facebook, Instagram, YouTube, news sites, online magazines, and more all show ads designed to lure users into spending money on products, from diet pills to swimsuits to skin products to protein shakes.

Many people present themselves on their personal social media in a way they think will make them, and their lives, look attractive and fun. It can become easy for people to think of themselves as the outward image that they project to online viewers. In 2013, women between ages eighteen and twenty-five completed an online experiment so that researchers could test the effect of media objectification. The women were shown fragrance ads that depicted either perfume bottles or a woman wearing lingerie. The women were then asked to describe themselves and choose an avatar image that would be seen either by an online audience or by no audience at all. Women who saw the woman wearing lingerie were more likely to self-objectify when they knew their avatar would be seen by an audience.

Objectification can be particularly damaging to young women as they develop their own identities. It can also affect older women, who may become convinced that they're not useful because they no longer fit the image of what the media perceive as sexy. Part of using social media is taking part in commenting on other people's posts, which can include comments about how people look. This reinforces objectification and the idea that appearance is what is important.

Social media interactions have led to some unhealthy trends, especially among teenagers. According to Dove:

> Social media has also introduced a new level of competitiveness into body-shape trends, with people keen to get "likes," "shares" and approving comments on their body-image selfies. Then there are the hashtag trends, memes and challenges – such as "is your waist narrower than a piece of A4 paper?" or "how many coins can you balance along your collarbone?" When their friends start sharing photos of themselves attempting the latest challenge, it's very hard for some young people to resist trying it too.[48]

Women may want to look like the models they see in advertisements. For teen girls, this might include posting photos of themselves on social media in an attempt to follow the media's idealized images of women.

For example, the A4 paper challenge, which started in China, encouraged women to hold up a piece of A4 printer paper (equivalent to standard US letter size) to see if their waists were smaller than the paper. Then they posted photos of this on social media. To be smaller than the paper, a person's waist would have to be 25 inches (63.5 cm) all the way around, which is unrealistic for many body types. The average American waist is 34 to 35 inches (86.4 to 88.9 cm). Social media trends such as this one are unhealthy and encourage an unrealistic body image. Even a high-profile Chinese fashion magazine editor called the A4 paper challenge "completely stupid."[49]

Social media is powerful in the world of fashion as it offers instant access to a large audience. People no longer have to wait for the latest edition of a print magazine to be published. Social media influencers— people who are paid to post about the latest products on platforms such as Instagram—can earn more than $80,000 per post. Candace Fremder, senior account director at a public relations company, said, "Influencers provide an immediate channel for brands to connect with their desired consumer in a unique and genuine way. In today's landscape, consumers are more likely to buy product recommended by a trusted and idolised social media star than product promoted via traditional advertising channels."[50] This might be great for the brands and the influencers, but it can have a negative effect on women viewing these social media posts. Jaywant Singh, a marketing professor at Kingston University in the United Kingdom, said, "Look at any of the top 10 Instagrammers—all you see is sexualised unattainable photoshopped images of sultry pouting teenagers with heaving cleavages and bare bottoms."[51] Singh believes these posts are successful because they make people feel inadequate and self-conscious, and then they

> "Creating and highlighting insecurities about the female body has . . . become central to many ad campaigns in the cosmetics and personal care industry."[53]
> – Jaywant Singh, marketing professor

suggest a product to make those people feel better. This makes people want to buy the products in these social media posts. Psychologists call this "compensatory consumption."[52] Singh added, "Creating and highlighting insecurities about the female body has, as a result, become central to many ad campaigns in the cosmetics and personal care industry."[53]

MODELS

If women viewing advertisements feel the effects of media objectification, how does it affect the models themselves who star in these advertisements? Renee Peters, a model from Nashville, explained, "Every day that you're working as a model, you're objectified somehow. You know, if it's just a simple term of you being a 'mannequin' or a 'model,' like you're not actually a person and you're just a vehicle for the clothing or the makeup or the hair."[54]

A study by researchers from Harvard University and Northeastern University found that 81 percent of models are underweight, while 62 percent of models had been told by their modeling agencies to lose weight. Not only is this unhealthy for the models themselves, it is unhealthy for the people viewing images of these models in advertisements and other media. Shivani Persad, a model from Trinidad and Tobago, said, "I've had instances where my agency has asked me to take down pictures from Instagram because they don't think it represents my best look. It's one thing when they ask you to change your body and you don't feel good about your body. But when you feel good about your body and then someone tells you that you shouldn't, it's a whole different story."[55]

> "I've had instances where my agency has asked me to take down pictures from Instagram because they don't think it represents my best look. It's one thing when they ask you to change your body and you don't feel good about your body. But when you feel good about your body and then someone tells you that you shouldn't, it's a whole different story."[55]
>
> *– Shivani Persad, a model from Trinidad and Tobago*

DIVERSITY IN MODELING

People are more likely to buy products if the advertisements feature models that look like them. So, it would be an advantage to companies to have advertisements that showcase a variety of genders, ethnicities, and body types. However,

Fashion shows primarily feature white, thin models. Women of color, plus-size women, and members of the LGBTQ community are underrepresented.

much of the fashion industry has lacked that diversity for years. For example, *The Fashion Spot*, a fashion website, analyzed the 2017 fashion runway shows in New York, Milan, London, and Paris. It concluded that more women of color walked the runway that year than ever before, but the majority of models were still white. Seventy-two percent of the models cast in all four cities combined were white, while 28 percent were women of color. Some designers still sent only white models down the runway. *The Fashion Spot* also analyzed print ads. In spring 2018, just 34 percent of the 541 models in these print ads were people of color.

Diandra Forrest, a model who is African American and albino, said in a *New York Times* article, "I've had pressure to change my look. I can recall comments about my skin or comments about my size or comments about my hair. The hair thing used to come up so much. It was insane: 'Why don't you just relax your hair or why don't you just perm it straight?' And I just said, 'No, I have curly hair. I love it.'"[56] Forrest added, "There are about two spots in a show for black girls out of maybe 50. Some shows don't even use black girls at all. When I was in Paris, I would speak to other models and I would have about 13 castings or 20 castings and the white girl would have like almost 40."[57]

As for body diversity, the statistics are bleak. During the fall 2017 fashion season, *The Fashion Spot* found that across the four cities, plus-size models made up just 0.43 percent of runway castings. However, the fashion brand J.Crew took a different approach for its fall 2017 show. Friends and family of people associated with the brand, as well as some employees, modeled its clothes. With that, J.Crew had one of the most race-, age- and size-inclusive shows that season. There is a similar lack of body diversity among models in print advertisements. Only ten models out of 541 were plus size in spring 2018 ads analyzed by *The Fashion Spot*. There is also little

"We have to all be seen. Not just some of us, not just ones who fit the transgender bill. Not just the streamline passable woman, or the plastic Kim [Kardashian] wannabe. We all have value and integrity. We deserve to be seen in mainstream media. . . . Our lives have purpose."[58]

– *Shay Neary, a plus-size transgender model*

representation of LGBTQ (lesbian, gay, bisexual, transgender, and queer) people—only four models in spring 2018 ad campaigns openly identified as transgender or non-binary. Representation matters, and models are more than objects to be gazed at; they are people who want to be seen as human beings. Shay Neary, a plus-size transgender model, said, "We have to all be seen. Not just some of us, not just ones who fit the transgender bill. Not just the streamline passable woman, or the plastic Kim [Kardashian] wannabe. We all have value and integrity. We deserve to be seen in mainstream media. . . . Our lives have purpose."[58]

Women are not only objectified in advertising. Women are underrepresented and misrepresented in movies, TV shows, and music. Objectification of women exists across the entertainment media industry.

CHAPTER THREE

HOW ARE WOMEN OBJECTIFIED IN ENTERTAINMENT MEDIA?

Entertainment media include television, film, video games, music, sports coverage, and online videos. They can be viewed on a TV at home, on a computer, in a movie theater, or streamed on a mobile device anywhere. Because entertainment media are so prevalent, they have a huge impact on how people view the world and themselves. As with other forms of media, women are repeatedly objectified and misrepresented in entertainment media.

WOMEN IN MOVIES

Women were only 24 percent of the protagonists featured in the top 100 US movies of 2017. Sixty-eight percent of all female characters in those movies were white, 16 percent were black, 7 percent were Asian, 7 percent were Latina, and 2 percent were of another race or ethnicity. Of the nine 2017 Oscar nominees for best picture, only two films—*Arrival* and *Hidden Figures*—were about women. Not only are women less visible in films, but when they are present, they are three times more likely than men to be shown in sexualized ways, such as having to wear sexually

Women are underrepresented as the protagonists in movies. *Hidden Figures*, **starring (from left) Octavia Spencer, Taraji P. Henson, and Janelle Monáe, was one of only two films about women that were nominated for the 2017 Oscar for best picture.**

appealing clothes or showing more body parts to the camera, such as their legs or breasts.

Women are often portrayed in movies as seeking romance or waiting for a stereotypical knight in shining armor to come rescue them. A 2017 study looked at the representation of women and girls ages six to twenty in movies. The study revealed that female teenagers were more likely than male teenagers to be shown as sexualized. This included female teens being four times more likely to be shown in sexually revealing clothing and more than twice as likely to be shown with partial nudity. Thirty-six percent of young female characters were shown engaging in stereotypically feminine chores such as housework or taking care of siblings. With stories focused on these stereotypes, school and studies were not featured for these female characters. Less than one-third of young girls were shown at school or doing homework. Only 12.2 percent of girls in the movies showed an interest in science, technology, engineering, and/or math (STEM). And only 7 percent of female characters had any professional aspirations. "Girls of today are dynamic and diverse. The entertainment industry continues to tell stories that bear little resemblance to the reality of today's girls and young women. Where are their intellectual pursuits? Their interest in STEM? Their desire for justice and equality? Those passions are not being shown with frequency in popular movies," said Stacy Smith, a professor at the University of Southern California who conducted the study.[59]

One way of analyzing the representation of women in a movie is by applying the Bechdel test. The test was named after its creator, American cartoonist Alison Bechdel. To pass the test, a film should feature at least two named female characters who speak to one another about something other than a man. It seems like a simple test, but many films do not pass. About 45 percent of films released in 2014 failed the Bechdel test. However, while the test is widely referenced, it does not always give an accurate representation of how well women are portrayed in films. For example, *Gravity*, which features a sole but important female protagonist, fails the test because she doesn't interact with any other female characters. However, *American Hustle* passes the Bechdel test, despite its heavy sexualization of female characters. Martha Lauzen, executive director of the Center for the Study of Women in Television and Film, suggests three additional questions to assess a movie. First, are the female characters central to the story? Second, do the female characters have agency, meaning do they take action themselves? And lastly, are the female characters multidimensional?

Additionally, screenwriters in Hollywood have come up with another tool that attempts to reduce the disparity between male and female roles in scripts. Christina Hodson is a screenwriter involved with Time's Up,

THE HEADLESS WOMEN OF HOLLYWOOD

In 2016, comedian Marcia Belsky created a Tumblr blog to highlight the dehumanization of women in Hollywood. On the blog, called *The Headless Women of Hollywood*, Belsky posted examples of posters that show women's bodies or body parts but not their heads and faces. She wrote, "By decapitating the woman, or fragmenting her body into decontextualized sexual parts, she becomes an unquestionably passive object to the male gaze. The question of her consent is removed completely alongside her head, and her purpose becomes solely that of being looked at by men obediently. Her value is that only of her sexual appeal to men, and not of her personhood."[1] Belsky's Tumblr includes posters from films that focus on sex such as *Showgirls* and *40 Days and 40 Nights*. But she also includes posters from movies that don't focus on sex yet still reduce women to body parts, such as a poster for the *Minions* movie. In her search through archives, Belsky found that the headless women trend wasn't in every movie poster, "maybe 10 out of 100 . . . but it's still a big number."[2]

1. "About The Headless Women Project," The Headless Women of Hollywood (blog), n.d. www.headlesswomenofhollywood.com.
2. Quoted in Hoai-Tran Bui, "'Headless Women of Hollywood' Blog Reveals Sexism of Movie Posters," USA Today, April 26, 2016. www.usatoday.com.

a Hollywood activist organization addressing gender inequality in the industry. Hodson had the idea to create a tool that could spot sexism and gender inequality in scripts before the scripts get turned into movies. Her idea was turned into reality in May 2018 by John August, the developer of a popular screenwriting app, Highland 2. Hodson's idea was added to the app, so the app can now analyze the number of male and female characters, and how much each speaks, in a script.

Even in animated movies, women are objectified. A 2008 study released by the Geena Davis Institute on Gender in Media found that in the majority of animated movies with female protagonists, such as *Snow White and the Seven Dwarfs* and *Sleeping Beauty,* female lead characters were portrayed with sexy, unrealistically shaped bodies. As part of the plotlines, the female protagonists were praised not for their actions or character, but for their appearance. Plus, these female characters' stories often focused on simply finding romance, and the characters lacked agency, needing to be saved by a prince. In 2012, *Brave* addressed some of these issues. The main character, Merida, has agency: She rebels against her parents who want to choose a husband for her, and she rescues herself. A 2016 report credited *Brave* (and Katniss, the lead character in *The Hunger Games*) for inspiring many girls to start practicing archery. The animated movies *Frozen* and *Moana* followed. *Frozen,* the highest-earning animated movie of all time, rejects the stereotypical romance-focused storyline, as it shows two sisters saving the day instead of waiting for a prince. *Moana* has been particularly celebrated for breaking the mold of Disney princesses with tiny waists. Rebecca Hains, author of *The Princess Problem: Guiding Our Girls through the Princess-Obsessed Years*, said, "It's clear to me that Disney has been listening to its critics. Having more heroines on screen who have a more average body type is really important, and it's a positive sign that Disney is taking some of these parental concerns to heart."[60]

WOMEN IN TV

In television, the statistics are better than in movies. Women were 42 percent of the TV characters on broadcast, network, and streaming programs between September 2016 and August 2017. Lauzen, of the Center for the Study of Women in Television and Film, said, "The industry's increasing openness to female-driven projects clearly is paying off in critically and commercially successful programs such as *The Handmaid's Tale* and *Big Little Lies*. Both series took home multiple trophies at this year's [2017] Emmys."[61]

But gender stereotypes are still prevalent on TV, including in children's shows. These stereotypes on TV and in movies teach children what the culture expects of them, according to Common Sense Media, a media education organization. Male characters are depicted as strong, funny, and emotionally restrained, whereas female characters are agreeable, virtuous, and care mainly about their physical appearances.

Animated movies have historically perpetuated stereotypes about women, including that women need to be saved by a prince. But several modern children's movies, such as Disney's *Frozen*, have rejected these stereotypes.

Female characters are also more likely to be shown crying. Preschoolers who are just beginning to identify as boys or girls watch media that show obvious masculine or feminine traits such as a superhero's big muscles or a princess's long hair. Common Sense Media said, "A lifetime of viewing stereotypical media becomes so ingrained it can ultimately affect kids' career choices, self-worth, relationships, and ability to achieve their full potential."[62] On TV shows and movies specifically aimed at children, boy characters outnumber girls by a ratio of roughly two to one. For example, the original *Paw Patrol*, a TV show about a group of rescue dogs and their ten-year-old leader, Ryder, featured six dogs, but only one was a girl. However, there are some examples of TV shows that show a balanced view of gender roles, such as *Daniel Tiger* and *Doc McStuffins*.

REALITY TV

The Bachelor. Keeping Up with the Kardashians. American Idol. Big Brother. Reality television makes up a huge part of the entertainment industry. But while these shows are billed as being reality, they are actually heavily manipulated by the producers, directors, and writers. "Certainly, reality TV is a very manipulated format where the basis of it is that real people are put into unreal situations to create a story," said J. Rupert Thompson, a director and producer who worked on *Big Brother.*[63] However, the Girl Scout Research Institute found that eight out of ten girls between ages eleven and seventeen who regularly watch reality TV believe that the shows are unscripted and entirely real.

Many of the women on reality TV shows are depicted as waiting for a man or scheming to beat one another in competition. Reality TV often emphasizes the value of women as being about how they look and what they wear—not what they think or what they do. According to a 2011 study by Parents Television Council, only 24 percent of what women said about themselves on reality TV was positive, and women were more critical than men when talking about themselves or other women. According to the Girl Scout survey, 38 percent of reality TV viewers said a girl's value is based on how she looks. And 28 percent of girls who viewed reality TV said they would rather be recognized for their beauty than for their values. Some reality TV stars maintain that they choose to objectify themselves, and this can be seen as positive. *Keeping Up with the Kardashians*, some argue, shows successful businesswomen who are positive role models. However, others say the show continues to objectify women, as, for example, much of the Kardashians' business

DR. DANA SCULLY

The representation of women on TV isn't all bad. In an example of how seeing positive female role models on TV can affect girls and women, a 2018 study showed that women who regularly watched *The X-Files* were significantly more likely to have considered going into a STEM career, majored in a STEM field in college, and worked in a STEM profession. Gillian Anderson starred as Dr. Dana Scully in *The X-Files*, a science-fiction drama that aired for nine seasons from 1993 to 2002, and again in 2016. According to the Geena Davis Institute on Gender in Media, scientists were often portrayed as white men in a lab, so Scully was an exception in the 1990s when she was the only prominent female STEM character on primetime television. Most women in the study also agreed that Scully is a "strong, smart, and intelligent character who increased their confidence to excel in a male-dominated profession." Anderson said that Scully "manifested a woman not yet depicted on TV and, as the fan response soon proved, a desperately needed role model for women of all ages, everywhere."

"The Scully Effect: I Want to Believe in STEM," Geena Davis Institute on Gender in Media, *n.d. www.seejane.org*

ventures focus on physical appearance with fashion and cosmetics. Kim Kardashian herself admits that she objectifies herself through her selfies, but she says it's because this gives her the ability to control her own image and brand.

NEWS AND POLITICS

The job of a news anchor is to present the latest news, interview people, and, in the case of women it seems, look glamorous. "It's disconcerting that there should be so much pressure to be überglamorous," said Katie Couric, a veteran news anchor who has been on many channels including CBS, NBC, and ABC. "I just don't think turning everyone into a Barbie doll is a good thing. It's very objectifying to women. I want to look more like the people watching me."[64] Meanwhile, male news anchors wear suits and ties and are often older than their female counterparts. TV journalist Jami Floyd said, "It's a cable phenomenon. There is a whole department devoted to makeup and hair at Fox, and it didn't matter which show you were on—the look was consistent. Their people seemed to put a lot of makeup on, and certainly a lot of eyelashes. The women wear skirts and heels."[65]

Many women in TV news have fought against this sexism. Several female TV hosts have sued their employers after being fired and replaced by younger hosts. In 2009, news reporter Shelly Sindland filed a complaint of gender and age discrimination against local Fox 61 in Connecticut after the news director joked about "Big Boob Fridays."[66] He said that when the women wore tighter shirts, the station got higher ratings. Sindland ended up reaching a settlement with the station. The Connecticut Commission on Human Rights and Opportunities (CHRO) said, "The information gathered through the investigative process [for Sindland's complaint] reveals that workplace conduct occurred that was unwelcome and offensive."[67]

> "It's a cable phenomenon. There is a whole department devoted to makeup and hair at Fox, and it didn't matter which show you were on—the look was consistent. Their people seemed to put a lot of makeup on, and certainly a lot of eyelashes. The women wear skirts and heels."[65]
>
> – Jami Floyd, TV journalist

The women who are being reported on by the news also face objectification. In 2008, Sarah Palin was the vice-presidential candidate for the Republican Party—a rare position for a woman. She and presidential candidate John McCain lost the election to Barack Obama. During the campaign, the Republican National Committee reportedly spent $150,000 improving Palin's wardrobe and appearance. A video clip of her wearing a swimsuit on the website YouTube received well over a million views, and *Time* magazine declared Palin a "sex symbol."[68]

Female politicians and other professional women often struggle to be taken seriously when they are being objectified and analyzed for what they wear and how they look. In 2005, researchers asked study participants to watch a videotaped woman who was dressed in either sexy or

REPRESENTATION IN NEWS MEDIA
IN 2018

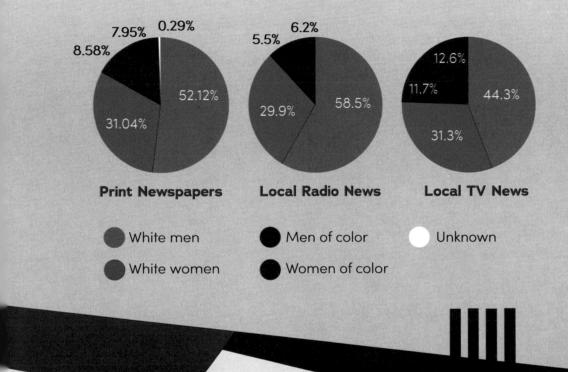

Print Newspapers

7.95% 0.29%
8.58%
52.12%
31.04%

Local Radio News

6.2%
5.5%
58.5%
29.9%

Local TV News

12.6%
11.7%
44.3%
31.3%

● White men   ● Men of color   ○ Unknown

● White women   ● Women of color

The Women's Media Center gathered information about how people were represented by race and gender on newsroom staffs in the United States in 2018. The center's research shows that there are many more men working in newsrooms than women. This means people are more likely to see male reporters on TV and to hear male voices on the radio. Additionally, people of color are greatly underrepresented in newsrooms.

"The Status of Women of Color in the U.S. News Media 2018," Women's Media Center, *March 6, 2018. www.womensmediacenter.com.*

business-like clothes and described as either a manager or a receptionist. The researchers discovered that participants were more negative toward the sexily dressed manager and rated her as less competent than the manager in business-like clothing. However, changing the receptionist's clothing had no effect on the participants' views of her competence. The researchers said, "These findings suggest that a sexy self-presentation harms women in high-, but not low-, status jobs."[69]

This objectification of women in media has an effect on young girls. Caroline Heldman, a politics professor at Occidental College, said in an interview for the 2011 documentary *Miss Representation* that when children are seven years old, around 30 percent of both boys and girls report wanting to become president. But by the time they're fifteen, the number of girls who say they would like to be president decreases dramatically compared with boys. Politics and leadership are considered natural for men, while women are discouraged from pursuing these kinds of roles. Women make up 51 percent of the US population, yet, as of 2018, only 20 percent of members of Congress were women.

SPORTS COVERAGE

Even though 40 percent of American athletes are female, only 4 percent of media coverage goes to women's sports, according to the Tucker Center for Research on Girls & Women in Sport at the University of Minnesota. Serena Williams, who has won more than twenty Grand Slam tennis championships and four Olympic gold medals, is not only a great athlete—she's also an example of the objectifying way that the media covers female athletes, particularly black women. In 2002, Otis Gibson, a newspaper columnist, commented on the outfit Williams was wearing to compete in the US Open. He said, "On some women [the catsuit] might look good. Unfortunately, some women aren't wearing it. On Serena, it only serves to accentuate a superstructure that is already bordering on the digitally enhanced and a rear end that I will attempt to sum up as

Tennis star Serena Williams has been a target for racism and sexism in the media, even though she is considered one of the greatest athletes of all time. Many women in sports media are subject to similar criticism.

discreetly as possible by simply referring to it as 'formidable.'"[70] In 2006, the *Telegraph* newspaper published a story written by Matthew Norman that said, "Generally, I'm all for chunky sports stars . . . but tennis requires a mobility Serena cannot hope to achieve while lugging around breasts that are registered to vote in a different US state from the rest of her."[71] And in *Rolling Stone* magazine in 2013, Stephen Roderick compared Williams and another tennis star, Maria Sharapova, saying, "Sharapova is tall, white and blond, and, because of that, makes more money in endorsements than Serena, who is black, beautiful and built like one of those monster trucks that crushes Volkswagens at sports arenas."[72]

Williams is often offensively compared to an animal in both traditional media and social media coverage. In 2012, David Leonard, a professor at

Washington State University, compiled the tweets that followed Williams' fifth Wimbledon championship win. He recorded a barrage of tweets comparing her to a gorilla, such as, "Today a giant gorilla escaped the zoo and won the womens title at Wimbledon… oh that was Serena Williams? My mistake."[73] On his blog, Leonard wrote, "The racism raining down on Serena's victory parade highlights the nature of white supremacy. . . . Her career has been one marred by the politics of hate, the politics of racism and sexism."[74]

Williams perseveres through this criticism, racism, and objectification. In 2015, she spoke about her own body image, saying, "I realized that you really have to learn to accept who you are and love who you are. I'm really happy with my body type, and I'm really proud of it. Obviously it works out for me. I talk about it all the time, how it was uncomfortable for someone like me to be in my body."[75]

"I realized that you really have to learn to accept who you are and love who you are. I'm really happy with my body type, and I'm really proud of it. Obviously it works out for me. I talk about it all the time, how it was uncomfortable for someone like me to be in my body."[75]
– Serena Williams, tennis champion

Williams is not the only female athlete objectified by the media. Many others find themselves defined by how they look instead of by their athletic accomplishments. After the 2016 Summer Olympics in Rio de Janeiro, Cynthia Frisby, a communications professor at the University of Missouri, analyzed the media coverage of male and female athletes during the 2012 and 2016 Olympics and compared the results. In 2012, she found sixty-nine cases of microaggressions, compared with ninety-six in 2016—an increase of nearly 40 percent. Microaggressions are described by Psychology Today as "everyday verbal, nonverbal, and environmental slights, snubs, or insults, whether intentional or unintentional, which communicate hostile, derogatory, or negative messages to target persons based solely upon their marginalized group membership."[76] Frisby identified several categories of microaggressions in her research, including sexual objectification, sexist and racist jokes, and a focus on the physical body and shape of the women. Some of the media coverage of Hungarian swimmer Katinka Hosszu praised her husband, who was also her coach, as "the man responsible" for her 2016 world-record performance, as if she was not responsible for her own success.[77] Frisby also found that "female athletes of color were more likely than white female athletes to receive microaggressions related to objectification, second-class citizenship (inferiority), restrictive gender roles, and commentary that relates to their body shape and body image."[78]

It seemed like things hadn't gotten much better by the 2018 Winter Olympics. Seventeen-year-old Chloe Kim won a gold medal in the women's snowboard halfpipe, becoming the youngest woman ever to win an Olympic snowboarding medal. On the Barstool Sports Sirius XM radio talk show *Dialed-In with Dallas Braden*, commentator Patrick Connor inappropriately called Kim a "little hot piece of ass."[79] As a result, Connor was fired from his other job at a San Francisco radio station—however, SiriusXM didn't take the same action.

VIDEO GAMES

A 2016 study examined the history of objectification of women in video games over a thirty-one-year period. Teresa Lynch, media communications researcher at Indiana University, compiled 571 playable female video game characters from 1989 to 2014. She examined them for signs of hypersexualization including nudity and unrealistic bodies, such as those with very narrow waists and enlarged breasts. Lynch found that sexualization peaked in 1995 before declining. In an example of this small improvement, Lara Croft in *Tomb Raider* went from wearing a midriff-bearing top and tiny shorts in the early editions of the game to a tank-top and pants in recent editions. Still, female characters in video games today are objectified more than male characters. According to Lynch's study, 47 percent of gamers are female, and they don't choose to play games that feature hypersexualized women. So, why do these games get made? Part of the issue is that the people working in the video game industry are mostly men—only 21 percent of respondents to an industry-wide game developer survey in 2017 identified as female. Along with being oversexualized, women are also frequently cast as victims in video games. Studies have suggested that exposure to severe violence against women in realistic video games normalizes the violence and even causes people to become less empathetic. Jeanne Brockmyer, a clinical child psychologist said, "The research is getting clearer that over the long term, people with more exposure to violent video games have demonstrated things like lower empathy to violence."[80]

> "The research is getting clearer that over the long term, people with more exposure to violent video games have demonstrated things like lower empathy to violence."[80]
>
> – Jeanne Brockmyer, clinical child psychologist

MUSIC

The music industry is another area rife with objectification. Women in music videos are often shown in suggestive and revealing clothing, while men are depicted as masculine and dominant. A 2011 study showed that female music artists were sexually objectified more often than male stars.

Music lyrics have also been studied. In a study of 160 songs, an average of 16 percent contained sexually degrading lyrics. That number rose to 70 percent in some specific genres, such as rap. Researchers identified a possible link between exposure to popular music and becoming sexually active at a young age. This could be because many teenagers accept, and even try to imitate, what they hear in objectifying lyrics. The researchers wrote, "These lyrics are likely to promote acceptance of women as sexual objects and men as pursuers of sexual conquest."[81]

ANALYZING OBJECTIFICATION

Media has a huge influence on people and, as research shows, it can have a detrimental effect on women and girls. "In many Western countries we are accustomed to being exposed to media images of undressed and sexy bodies often used as decorative objects or instruments to attract new consumers," said Francesca Guizzo, who conducted a study in Italy about how people feel about women being objectified in media.[82] Guizzo found that people who regularly watch media in which women are objectified were less likely realize it's not okay to objectify a woman's body or even to react to this objectification. During the study, Guizzo's team showed some participants a television clip in which women were sexually objectified. Other participants saw the same clip with a commentary explaining why the footage degraded women, and others watched a nature documentary instead. The women who watched the objectifying clip with the commentary were most likely to feel angry about how the women were treated, and they were more willing to support protest actions such as a rally or petition. Guizzo found that men did not react the same way. "The overall pattern of results suggests that the chronic exposure to objectifying media might lead to the dangerous assumption that such female portrayal is the norm, thus further reducing people's likelihood to react," Guizzo said.[83] To combat this, she said, more entertainment media needs to be critically analyzed to show the instances in which women are being objectified. There are initiatives and organizations, such as the Geena Davis Institute on Gender in Media, that are working to make a difference and to persuade directors and writers to produce movies and television shows that are more representative of real women.

CHAPTER FOUR

WHAT DOES THE FUTURE HOLD FOR WOMEN IN MEDIA?

There has been an increase in awareness and a backlash against objectification, with celebrities, audiences, organizations, and the media industry itself challenging unrealistic and limiting portrayals of women in advertising and entertainment media. In the future, it is hoped that advertising and media will be more inclusive and that people will no longer be objectified. But for that to happen, consumers need to speak out when they see negative portrayals of women in media, and companies need to listen. One solution could be new legislation to govern media, such as the standards used by the advertising industry in the United Kingdom.

ADVERTISING STANDARDS

In the United Kingdom, there are advertising standards in place to reduce objectification. The Advertising Standards Authority (ASA), enforces these rules. In 2015, it banned an ad in the magazine *Vogue UK* from fashion brand Miu Miu. The ASA said the model in the ad had a "youthful appearance, was wearing very minimal makeup, and clothes that appeared to be slightly too large," which gave the impression that

Women are repeatedly objectified in magazines and print advertisements. Some countries, such as the United Kingdom, have stricter rules than the United States regarding sexualized images in print advertisements.

she was younger than sixteen.[84] The ASA said the composition of the photo was problematic: "She was posed reclining on a bed, looking up directly to the camera through a partially opened door, which gave her an air of vulnerability and the image a voyeuristic feel. We considered that the crumpled sheets and her partially opened mouth also enhanced the impression that her pose was sexually suggestive."[85]

In 2016, the ASA banned an ad for the British clothing brand Jack Wills for using sexualized images and text that were inappropriate for young people. The brand's catalog included images of male and female models on a bed together, wearing only underwear, with text stating, "Whatever your choice, you can be sure it's what's underneath that counts" and "Midnight mischief."[86] The ASA said, "Because we understood that younger teenagers could have both direct and indirect access to the catalogue, and because we considered the images and text were sufficiently sexualised to be inappropriate for that audience, we concluded that the ad was irresponsible and that it breached the Code."[87] The ASA's code says it "does not prevent marketers from using images of children but they should do so in a socially responsible manner."[88] Jack Wills, however, disagreed with the ASA in this case, saying, "The images were not sexualized or provocative and did not imply sexual activity in any way."[89]

In 2018, the ASA proposed new standards on advertisements that feature stereotypical gender roles or characteristics. Ella Smillie of the Committees of Advertising Practice, a sister organization to the ASA, said: "Some gender stereotypes in ads can contribute to harm for adults and children by limiting how people see themselves, how others see them, and potentially restricting the life decisions they take. The introduction of a new advertising rule from 2018 will help advertisers to know where to draw the line on the use of acceptable and unacceptable stereotypes."[90]

In the United States, there aren't such stringent rules. The Federal Trade Commission, which oversees advertising standards, says, "Advertising must tell the truth and not mislead consumers. In addition, claims must be substantiated."[91] But there are no rules governing how women are portrayed in the advertisements. In 2016, US lawmakers proposed legislation that would create a regulatory framework for advertisements to ensure they aren't deceiving. In other words, the legislation would stop advertisers from airbrushing their models. But this proposal has not yet been passed into law. Still, some companies have started adopting their own rules against airbrushing and narrow views of body sizes, realizing that consumers demand more honesty and reality in advertising and media.

WHAT ABOUT OBJECTIFICATION OF MEN?

During the 2016 Summer Olympics in Rio de Janeiro, it seemed all eyes were on the men. Headlines across various media outlets included "2016 Rio Olympics: The U.S. Men Gymnasts, Ranked by Ab Appeal!" and "All the Shirtless Ryan Lochte Photos You Could Ever Possibly Want."[1] But is this objectification okay? If the headlines were about women, they would have definitely been called out as sexist and demeaning. So surely that's the same if they're about men? The difference is, people are also encouraged to pay attention to male Olympians' athletic accomplishments, and these men are valued for their athletic abilities regardless of whether they're seen as conventionally attractive. *Guardians of the Galaxy* actor Chris Pratt has addressed objectification of men, saying, "I think it's appalling that for a long time only women were objectified, but I think if we really want to advocate for equality, it's important to even things out."[2] However, activist Jean Kilbourne disagrees that men should be equally objectified: "Believe me, this is not the kind of equality I'm fighting for. I don't want them to do this to men any more than to women."[3]

1. Katie Mettler, "'Hottest Olympic Dudes'? 'Ab Appeal'? It's Objectification When It's about Women. What about Men?" The Washington Post, August 9, 2016. www.washingtonpost.com.
2. Ben Child, "Jurassic World's Chris Pratt: Equality Means Objectifying Men Too," The Guardian, June 19, 2015. www.theguardian.com.
3. "What About the Objectification of Men?," Collective Shout, April 17, 2018. www.collectiveshout.org.

POSITIVE ADVERTISING CAMPAIGNS

Cosmetics company Dove launched a marketing campaign in 2004 called Campaign for Real Beauty, with the goal of promoting positive body images. Dove produced ads featuring everyday women instead of professional models. It also had an ad showing how Photoshop turns models into the impossible ideal typically shown in marketing images. Despite a largely positive campaign, the brand has not been without its critics. In 2017, Dove launched its "Real Beauty Bottles." The plastic body wash bottles were available in six different shapes, each of which were supposed to represent different women's body types, from hourglass to pear-shaped. The advertisement included the line, "Real beauty breaks molds."[92] On its website, Dove said, "Just like women, we wanted to show

The Campaign for Real Beauty from Dove Cosmetics is an example of an advertising campaign focused on positive body image. The campaign celebrated its ten-year anniversary in 2014.

that our iconic bottle can come in all shapes and sizes, too."[93] However, critics suggested that asking a woman to choose her body type, or perhaps her aspirational body type, from a lineup of bottles in a store is a body-image issue in itself. It turns women's bodies into objects. A user on Twitter said, "Like, I just want to [use] my body wash, not be reminded that I'm pear shaped. Women don't need to be categorized all the time."[94]

In the United Kingdom, Sport England launched a campaign in 2015 called This Girl Can to normalize images of girls and women engaging in sports and to increase women's involvement in sports. The campaign showed women participating in sports "regardless of size, shape or ability."[95] The campaign's ads had women saying things like "I jiggle therefore I am" and "I kick balls—deal with it."[96] Sport England reported an increase of almost 230,000 women and girls older than age sixteen participating in sports between 2015 and 2016. The campaign featured a sixty-seven-year-old swimmer, a woman running with a blade after losing a leg, and a roller derby player.

Always, a feminine hygiene company, also designed a campaign aimed to empower girls. With the #LikeAGirl campaign launched in 2014, Always said on its website that it wanted to empower young women. Always added that it wanted to change statistics, such as the fact that at puberty, "50% of girls feel paralyzed by the fear of failure, with 80% of girls feeling that societal pressure to be perfect drives this fear of failure."[97] Judy John, an advertising executive who worked on the #LikeAGirl campaign, said, "The idea was explained as: 'like a girl' has been around forever and is used in derogatory ways, let's change the meaning of it. From that day on we started to build on that idea."[98] For the campaign, filmmaker Lauren Greenfield produced a film about what it means to run, throw, and fight "like a girl."[99] The result revealed that between puberty and adulthood, many women interpret the phrase "like a girl" to mean weakness and vanity. In the film, when teenagers and adults are told to run or throw like a girl, they act silly and flip their hair, and they don't make an effort to throw a ball properly. But when young girls are asked to perform the same tasks "like a girl," they run with strength and put all their energy into the activity. This shows that "like a girl" is a positive phrase to the younger girls. The advertising campaign aimed to make all women feel proud to be "like a girl."

SAYING NO TO AIRBRUSHING

As well as using more realistic images of women, companies have started to reduce the amount of digital manipulation used in their advertising.

CVS Pharmacy is one company that has pledged to stop using digitally altered photos in its advertising. While some other companies have made similar promises, airbrushed photos are overall still the norm in advertising.

In 2018, CVS Pharmacy pledged to stop materially altering all of the imagery associated with its beauty products—in stores, on its website, and on social media. CVS defines *materially altering* as "changing or enhancing a person's shape, size, proportion, skin or eye color, wrinkles, or any other individual characteristics."[100] CVS has also asked brands it sells, such as Maybelline and L'Oreal, to follow its lead or to clearly and visibly label retouched images as modified.

CVS isn't the first company to cut out Photoshop. In 2016, Pirelli published a non-airbrushed calendar for the first time and asked women, including actors Nicole Kidman, Julianne Moore, and Helen Mirren, to pose unfiltered. Photographer Peter Lindbergh said of the project, "We see all these people today who all want to be perfect and young. My thought was, 'Why don't we do a calendar with women ready to go without much makeup, to be as they are?' For me, beauty is someone who can say yes to herself."[101] In 2014, online fashion retailer ModCloth also took a pledge against altering images. It said it would not "change the shape, size, proportion, color and/or remove/enhance the physical features" of models in its advertisements.[102] In 2014, lingerie brand Aerie launched its Aerie Real marketing campaign, featuring completely unaltered models. Aerie's advertising featured models with tattoos, freckles, and scars that would normally be digitally removed before their photographs made it into advertisements. In 2018, Aerie started using a range of women to model its lingerie, including a woman in a wheelchair, a woman with a diabetic pump, and a model with Down syndrome.

In 2012, then-eighth-grader Julia Bluhm launched an online petition asking *Seventeen* magazine to include at least one unaltered photo spread in each issue. "We should focus on people's personalities, not just how they look," she said.[103] Bluhm's petition got 80,000 signatures. *Seventeen* editor Ann Shoket

> "We should focus on people's personalities, not just how they look."[103]
> – *Julia Bluhm, eighth grade*

agreed with the petition. But she went further and issued a statement promising that across the whole magazine, *Seventeen* would not alter photos and would include only images of "real girls and models who are healthy."[104]

Verily, an online fashion and lifestyle magazine, launched in 2012 with a no-Photoshop pledge. On its website, *Verily* states:

> *Whereas other magazines photoshop to achieve the "ideal" body type and skin, we firmly believe that the unique features of women—be it*

crows feet, freckles, or a less-than-rock-hard body—contribute to their beauty and don't need to be removed or changed with Photoshop. Therefore, we never alter the body or facial structure of our models, remove wrinkles or birthmarks, or change the texture of their skin. We aim to show everyone at their best, but also firmly believe that "your best" is not "a work of fiction."[105]

CELEBRITIES SPEAK OUT

More female celebrities are publicly opposing misrepresentations of themselves in media. Kerry Washington, an actor known for her starring role in the television show *Scandal*, has spoken out against her body being Photoshopped on more than one occasion. "It felt strange to look at a picture of myself that is so different from what I look like when I look in the mirror. It's an unfortunate feeling," she said.[106] When Washington was featured on the cover of *InStyle* magazine in March 2015, readers responded with outrage that her skin seemed to have been lightened. Editors of the magazine responded to the criticism by saying they didn't deliberately lighten Washington's skin but that it appeared that way likely because of the lighting used at the photoshoot.

> "It felt strange to look at a picture of myself that is so different from what I look like when I look in the mirror. It's an unfortunate feeling."[106]
> – Kerry Washington, actor

Model and actor Zendaya spoke out against photos of herself that were digitally altered in the November 2015 edition of *Modeliste* magazine. "[I] was shocked when I found my 19 year old hips and torso quite manipulated. These are the things that make women self conscious, that create the unrealistic ideals of beauty that we have," she said.[107] The magazine quickly removed the altered images from its website and replaced them with the untouched original photos.

Research shows that movies with female protagonists succeed at the box office. *Star Wars: The Last Jedi* was one of the top three highest-grossing films in 2017; all three of those films had female lead characters.

IMPROVEMENTS IN REPRESENTATION

Star Wars is a classic movie franchise that started in 1977 with *A New Hope* and was still going in 2018 with *Solo*. In 2018, author and film lecturer Becca Harrison studied the *Star Wars* films to figure out which ones include the most screen time for female characters. Harrison posted her results on Twitter, revealing that the top three films to give women the most screen time are *The Last Jedi*, *The Force Awakens*, and *Rogue One*. All three have female-centric stories. The three films are also the highest-earning of all the *Star Wars* films so far. Statistics show that it isn't just the *Star Wars* franchise that sees movies with female-focused storylines earning more money. *Mic*, a news website, looked at the top twenty-five highest-earning films each year from 2006 to mid-October 2015. *Mic* concluded that movies with female protagonists made an average of $126.1 million, compared with the films with male protagonists, which made an average of $80.6 million. The Geena Davis Institute on Gender in Media studied the top 100 films from 2017 and found that films starring a woman made 38 percent more at the box office than films starring a man. The top three highest-grossing US films in 2017 all had female leads: *Star Wars: The Last Jedi*, *Beauty and the Beast*, and *Wonder Woman*. In 2018, the BBC looked at the Oscar-nominated films for that year. It also concluded that movies with a clearly definable female lead made more money—they were 33 percent more profitable than male-led films.

CAMPAIGNS TO INCREASE AWARENESS

Many organizations exist to bring about change in the media world and to improve the representation of women. About Face "arms girls with the knowledge and tools they need to fight back against a culture that diminishes and disempowers them," according to its website.[108] The organization publishes galleries of objectifying ads from brands such as American Apparel and Victoria's Secret, and it teaches teenagers to interpret media critically.

The Geena Davis Institute on Gender in Media was started by Academy Award–winning actor Geena Davis in 2004. The institute educates and influences both content creators and audiences about the importance of seeking gender balance, challenging stereotypes, and creating role models in media for children. Paula Kerger, president and

CEO of PBS, said, "We're proud to partner with the Geena Davis Institute on Gender in Media as we work to empower girls. It's so important that young girls have examples of women on-screen that are smart, resilient, and inspiring, so they can grow up to reach their full potential."[109] In 2016, the institute launched a tool, the Geena Davis Inclusion Quotient (GD-IQ), to automatically analyze and calculate the representation of women and other demographic groups in entertainment media.

> "It's so important that young girls have examples of women on-screen that are smart, resilient, and inspiring, so they can grow up to reach their full potential."[109]
> – Paula Kerger, president and CEO of PBS

These organizations, the voluntary rules that magazines and brands have put in place, and an increase in representation of women in media are starting to make a difference. In 2017, the Geena Davis Institute on Gender in Media found that 66 percent of women said they have switched off films or TV shows that they felt showed negative female stereotypes, and one in four women said that they had stopped watching a film or TV show because there weren't enough female characters. This figure was higher among millennial women (born between 1981 and 1996)—46 percent of them stopped watching media that didn't have enough female characters.

As positive representation of women in media increases and objectification decreases, women and girls in the future may be able to watch more movies and TV shows and read more magazines that do not objectify women. Instead, media will be truly reflective of the real world, featuring women with careers that others can aspire to and celebrating women's successes instead of their sexiness.

SOURCE NOTES

INTRODUCTION: WHAT IS OBJECTIFICATION?

1. Quoted in Jonathan Evans, "The NSFW History of American Apparel's Ads." *Esquire*, October 11, 2017. www.esquire.com.

2. Quoted in Rose Hackman, "Are You Beach Body Ready? Controversial Weight Loss Ad Sparks Varied Reactions," *The Guardian*, June 27, 2015. www.theguardian.com.

3. Quoted in Stephanie Pappas, "Brain Sees Men as Whole, Women as Parts," *Live Science*, July 24, 2012. www.livescience.com.

4. Quoted in Pappas, "Brain Sees Men as Whole, Women as Parts."

5. Quoted in *Miss Representation*. Directed by Jennifer Siebel Newsom, The Representation Project, 2011.

6. Quoted in *Embrace*. Directed by Taryn Brumfitt, Body Image Movement, 2016.

7. Quoted in *Miss Representation*.

8. "Not an Object: On Sexualization and Exploitation of Women and Girls," *UNICEF USA*, May 9, 2016. www.unicefusa.org.

CHAPTER 1. HAVE WOMEN ALWAYS BEEN OBJECTIFIED?

9. "Elizabeth Cady Stanton, 'Our Girls' (Winter 1880)," *Voices of Democracy*, n.d. www.voicesofdemocracy.umd.edu.

10. Jennifer Nelson, *Airbrushed Nation*. Berkeley, CA: Seal Press, 2012. p. 8.

11. Quoted in Nelson, *Airbrushed Nation*, p. 12.

12. Quoted in Juliann Sivulka, *Ad Women: How They Impact What We Need, Want, and Buy*. Amherst, New York: Prometheus Books, 2009. p. 296.

13. Quoted in Sivulka, *Ad Women*, p. 296.

14. Quoted in Sivulka, *Ad Women*, p. 296.

15. Quoted in Sivulka, *Ad Women*, p. 296.

16. Patricia Donovan, "Study Finds Marked Rise in Intensely Sexualized Images of Women, Not Men," *University at Buffalo News Center*, August 10, 2011. www.buffalo.edu.

17. Bosley Crowther, "LOOK AT MARILYN!: A Lot Is Seen of Miss Monroe (As a Symbol) in 'The Seven Year Itch,'" *New York Times*, June 12, 1955. www.nytimes.com.

18. Crowther, "LOOK AT MARILYN!"

19. Richard Meryman, "Great Interviews of the 20th Century: Marilyn Monroe Interviewed by Richard Meryman," *The Guardian*, September 14, 2007. www.theguardian.com.

20. *Dr. No*. Directed by Terence Young, Eon Productions, 1962.

21. Quoted in Rachael Sampson, "Film Theory 101 – Laura Mulvey: The Male Gaze Theory," *Film Inquiry*, May 3, 2018. www.filminquiry.com.

22. Quoted in Kelly Wallace, "Teens Spend 9 Hours a Day Using Media, Report Says," *CNN*, November 3, 2015. www.cnn.com.

23. Joe Perticone, "Here's What Hillary Looks Like After Paying $600 for a Haircut That Shut Down an Entire Salon," *Independent Journal Review*, July 30, 2015. www.ijr.com.

24. Robin Givhan, "Hillary Clinton's Tentative Dip into New Neckline Territory," *Washington Post*, July 20, 2007. www.washingtonpost.com.

25. Quoted in Emily Chan, "Canada's Next PM Makes Headlines Worldwide," *CTVNews*, October 20, 2015. www.ctvnews.ca.

26. Neha Prakash, "Canada's Hot New Prime Minister Has the Internet Sweating Maple Syrup," *Mashable*, October 20, 2015. www.mashable.com.

27. Georgina Dent, "Why It's Ok To Objectify Trudeau But Not Theresa May," *Marie Claire*, March 30, 2017. www.marieclaire.com.au.

28. "The Status of Women in the U.S. Media 2017," *Women's Media Center*, March 21, 2017. www.womensmediacenter.com.

29. Quoted in "Women's Media Center Report: Women Journalists Report Less News than Men; TV Gender Gap Most Stark," *Women's Media Center*, March 22, 2017. www.womensmediacenter.com.

30. Quoted in "Women of Color, Who Are Underrepresented in U.S. News Media, Share Frustrations, Triumphs in Special Report," *Women's Media Center*, March 6, 2018. www.womensmediacenter.com.

31. "Geena Davis Institute on Gender in Media," *Geena Davis Institute on Gender in Media*, n.d., www.seejane.org.

CHAPTER 2. HOW ARE WOMEN OBJECTIFIED IN ADVERTISING?

32. Quoted in Rachel Shields, "By 12, Girls Have Seen 77,500 Ads. And Does It Make Them Happy?" *The Independent*, October 7, 2007. www.independent.co.uk.

33. Quoted in Shields, "By 12, Girls Have Seen 77,500 Ads."

34. Quoted in Maggie Mallon, "A New Study Shows Advertisements Are So Sexist, Men Get 7 Times as Many Speaking Roles as Women," *Glamour*, June 23, 2017. www.glamour.com.

35. "Gender Bias in Advertising," *Geena Davis Institute on Gender in Media*, January 22, 2018. www.seejane.org.

36. Quoted in Katya Foreman, "The Bra: An Uplifting Tale," *BBC Culture*, February 20, 2015. www.bbc.com.

37. Linda Papadopoulos, *Sexualisation of Young People Review*, 2010. dera.ioe.ac.uk.

38. J.D. Reed and Wendy Cole, "Return of the Body Snatcher," *Time*, September 1989. www.time.com.

39. "Going Too Far With the Winfrey Diet," *New York Times*, August 20, 1989. www.nytimes.com.

41. Melissa Wells, *Instagram*, June 22, 2016. www.instagram.com.

42. Quoted in Alisa Wolfson, "Why Companies like Dove Are Ditching Photoshop in Their Ad Campaigns," *Moneyish*, June 26, 2018. www.moneyish.com.

43. Quoted in Valeriya Safronova, Joanna Nikas, and Natalia V. Osipova, "What It's Truly Like To Be a Fashion Model," *New York Times*, September 5, 2017. www.nytimes.com.

44. Quoted in RedrumBros, "Miller Light Catfight - Banned Commercial," *YouTube*, May 28, 2007. www.youtube.com.

45. Mina Enayati-Uzeta, "Gen Z Watches Super Bowl Ads," *3 Percent Movement*, February 15, 2018. www.3percentmovement.com.

46. Enayati-Uzeta, "Gen Z Watches Super Bowl Ads."

47. "A Sweet, Smoky Taste...With More Than a Hint of Sexism," *About Face*, April 12, 2018. www.about-face.org.

48. "Help Your Child Defy Body Trends and Beat the Body-Shamers," *Dove*, January 11, 2016. www.dove.com.

49. Quoted in Didi Kirsten Tatlow, "On Social Media in China, Size 0 Doesn't Make the Cut," *New York Times*, March 19, 2016. www.nytimes.com.

50. Quoted in Sarah Young, "Inside the Weird and Wonderful World of Fashion Bloggers Who Can Earn up to £60,000 per Instagram Post," *The Independent*, October 7, 2016. www.independent.co.uk.

51. Quoted in Olivia Petter, "How Companies Are Using Women's Insecurities to Make More Money," *The Independent*, August 23, 2017. www.independent.co.uk.

52. Quoted in Petter, "How Companies Are Using Women's Insecurities to Make More Money."

53. Quoted in Petter, "How Companies Are Using Women's Insecurities to Make More Money."

54. Quoted in Safronova, Nikas, and Osipova, "What It's Truly Like To Be a Fashion Model."

55. Quoted in Safronova, Nikas, and Osipova, "What It's Truly Like To Be a Fashion Model."

56. Quoted in Safronova, Nikas, and Osipova, "What It's Truly Like To Be a Fashion Model."

57. Quoted in Safronova, Nikas, and Osipova, "What It's Truly Like To Be a Fashion Model."

58. Quoted in Cordelia Tai, "Transgender Plus-Size Model Shay Neary Just Booked a Historic Campaign," *The Fashion Spot*, December 22, 2016. www.thefashionspot.com.

CHAPTER 3. HOW ARE WOMEN OBJECTIFIED IN ENTERTAINMENT MEDIA?

59. Quoted in "The Future Is Female, Just Not in Film: Image of Girls in Popular Movies Bears Little Resemblance to Reality," *USC Annenberg School for Communication and Journalism*, November 10, 2017. annenberg.usc.edu.

60. Quoted in Tom Brook, "The Controversy behind Disney's Groundbreaking New Princess," *BBC Culture*, November 28, 2016. www.bbc.com.

61. Martha Lauzen, "What We Know for Sure about Women in Television," *Women's Media Center*, September 28, 2017. www.womensmediacenter.com.

62. Caroline Knorr, "Gender Stereotypes Are Messing with Your Kid," *Common Sense Media*, June 19, 2017. www.commonsensemedia.org.

63. Quoted in Michael Ventre, "Just How Real Are Reality TV Shows?" *Today*, April 15, 2009. www.today.com.

64. Quoted in Judy Bachrach, "The Complicated History Behind the Hair and Makeup of Female News Anchors," *Allure*, November 20, 2017. www.allure.com.

65. Quoted in Bachrach, "The Complicated History Behind the Hair and Makeup of Female News Anchors."

66. Quoted in Andrew Gauthier, "Veteran Reporter Shelly Sindland Close to Finalizing Discrimination Settlement with WTIC," *Adweek TVSpy*, January 6, 2011. www.adweek.com.

67. Quoted in Teri Buhl, "Former Fox 61 Reporter Sindland Settles Discrimination Case Against Courant Publisher," *CTWatchdog*, January 6, 2011. www.ctwatchdog.com.

68. Bill Tancer, "Searching for Sarah Palin's 'Hot Photos,'" *Time*, September 2, 2008. www.time.com.

69. Peter Glick, Sadie Larsen, Cathryn Johnson, and Heather Branstiter, "Evaluations of Sexy Women in Low- and High-Status Jobs," *Psychology of Women Quarterly*, vol. 29, no. 4, December 2005. pp. 389–395.

70. Quoted in Jen Desmond-Harris, "Serena Williams Is Constantly the Target of Disgusting Racist and Sexist Attacks," *Vox*, March 11, 2015. www.vox.com.

71. Quoted in Desmond-Harris, "Serena Williams Is Constantly the Target."

72. Quoted in Desmond-Harris, "Serena Williams Is Constantly the Target."

73. Quoted in Desmond-Harris, "Serena Williams Is Constantly the Target."

74. Quoted in Desmond-Harris, "Serena Williams Is Constantly the Target."

75. Quoted in Ben Rothenberg, "Tennis's Top Women Balance Body Image With Ambition," *New York Times*, July 10, 2015. www.nytimes.com.

76. Derald Wing Sue, "Microaggressions: More than Just Race," *Psychology Today*, November 17, 2010. www.psychologytoday.com.

77. Quoted in Lindsay Gibbs, "Media Coverage of Female Athletes Is Getting More Sexist." *ThinkProgress*, July 14, 2017. www.thinkprogress.org.

78. Quoted in Gibbs, "Media Coverage of Female Athletes Is Getting More Sexist."

79. Quoted in Laura Wagner, "Barstool Radio Host Can't Resist Calling 17-Year-Old Olympian Chloe Kim A 'Little Hot Piece of Ass,'" *Deadspin*, February 13, 2018. www.deadspin.com.

80. Quoted in Nick Bilton, "Looking at Link Between Violent Video Games and Lack of Empathy." *New York Times*, June 15, 2014. www.nytimes.com.

81. Steven C. Martino, Rebecca L. Collins, Marc N. Elliott, Amy Strachman, David E. Kanouse, and Sandra H. Berry, "Exposure to Degrading Versus Nondegrading Music Lyrics and Sexual Behavior Among Youth," *Pediatrics*, The American Academy of Pediatrics, April 11, 2006.

82. Quoted in Zara Barrie, "Watching TV Shows That Degrade Women Makes You Sexist," *Elite Daily*, January 6. 2017. www.elitedaily.com.

83. Francesca Guizzo, "Women as Decorative Accessories: Keep Silent or Take a Stance?" ScienceDaily, January 4, 2017. www.sciencedaily.com.

CHAPTER 4. WHAT DOES THE FUTURE HOLD FOR WOMEN IN MEDIA?

84. Quoted in Rebecca Sullivan, "Miu Miu Ad Banned for 'Sexualizing Young Women,'" *News.com.au*, May 8, 2015. www.news.com.au.

85. Quoted in Sullivan, "Miu Miu Ad Banned for 'Sexualizing Young Women.'"

86. Quoted in "Jack Wills Ad Banned by Advertising Standards Authority over 'Irresponsible' Sexualised Images," *The Telegraph*, June 1, 2016. www.telegraph.co.uk.

87. Quoted in "Jack Wills Ad Banned by Advertising Standards Authority."

88. "Children: Sexual Imagery," *Advertising Standards Authority / Committees of Advertising Practice*, January 2, 2018. www.asa.org.uk.

89. Quoted in "Jack Wills Ad Banned by Advertising Standards Authority."

90. "New Rule to Ban Harmful Gender Stereotypes Next Year," *Advertising Standards Authority / Committees of Advertising Practice*, December 14, 2017. www.asa.org.uk.

91. "Advertising and Marketing on the Internet: Rules of the Road," *Federal Trade Commission*, March 19, 2018. www.ftc.gov.

92. Quoted in Ian Bogost, "How Dove Ruined Its Body Image," *The Atlantic*, May 9, 2017. www.theatlantic.com.

93. "Celebrating Beauty Diversity with Limited Edition Body Washes," *Dove*, n.d., www.dove.com.

94. Quoted in Abha Bhattarai, "Why Ladies Didn't Love Dove's Latest Gender-Empowering Ad Stunt," *Washington Post*, May 9, 2017. www.washingtonpost.com.

95. Quoted in Laura Hills, "This Girl Can Has Really Made a Difference to Women in Sport," *The Conversation*, June 21, 2018. www.theconversation.com.

96. Quoted in Hills, "This Girl Can Has Really Made a Difference to Women in Sport."

97. "Our Epic Battle #LikeAGirl." *Always*, n.d. www.always.com.

98. Quoted in "Case Study: Always #LikeAGirl." *D&AD*, n.d. www.dandad.org.

99. Quoted in Hannah Goldberg, "Like a Girl: New Always Ad Plays on Gender Stereotypes #LikeAGirl." *Time*, June 26, 2014. www.time.com.

100. Quoted in Vanessa Friedman, "Airbrushing Meets the #MeToo Movement. Guess Who Wins," *New York Times*, January 15, 2018. www.nytimes.com.

101. Quoted in Ruth La Ferla, "Pirelli's Reality Check: Portraying Beauty at Any Age," *New York Times*, November 30, 2016. www.nytimes.com.

102. Quoted in Alicia Adamczyk, "ModCloth Is First Retailer to Sign Anti-Photoshop Pledge," *Forbes*, September 3, 2014. www.forbes.com.

103. Quoted in Elise Hu, "'Seventeen' Magazine Takes No-Photoshop Pledge After 8th-Grader's Campaign," *National Public Radio*, July 5, 2012. www.npr.org.

104. Quoted in Hu, "'Seventeen' Magazine Takes No-Photoshop Pledge."

105. "About Us," *Verily*, May 18, 2015. www.verilymag.com.

106. Isabel Calkins, "13 Times Celebrities Called Out Magazines Over Retouching." *Cosmopolitan*, April 11, 2016. www.cosmopolitan.com.

107. "Zendaya 'Shocked' to Find Herself Photoshopped," *CNN*, October 22, 2015. www.cnn.com.

108. "About Us," *About Face*, n.d. www.about-face.org.

109. "About Us," *Geena Davis Institute on Gender in Media*, n.d. www.seejane.org.

FOR FURTHER **RESEARCH**

BOOKS

Theresa Carilli and Jane Campbell, *Challenging Images of Women in the Media: Reinventing Women's Lives*. Lanham, MD: Lexington Books, 2012.

Carolyn Cocca, *Superwomen: Gender, Power, and Representation*. New York: Bloomsbury Publishing Inc., 2016.

Marquita Marie Gammage, *Representations of Black Women in Media*. New York: Routledge, 2016.

Alicia Malone, *Backwards and in Heels: The Past, Present and Future of Women Working in Film*. Coral Gables, FL: Mango Pub. Group, 2018.

INTERNET SOURCES

Sara Boboltz and Kimberly Yam, "Why On-Screen Representation Actually Matters," *Huffington Post*, February 24, 2017. www.huffingtonpost.com.

Hoai-Tran Bui, "'Headless Women of Hollywood' Blog Reveals Sexism of Movie Posters," *USA Today,* April 26, 2016. www.usatoday.com.

Sarah Ruiz-Grossman, "U.S. Newsrooms Have Dismal Representation of Women of Color," *Huffington Post,* March 8, 2018. www.huffingtonpost.com.

"The Scully Effect: I Want to Believe in STEM," *Geena Davis Institute on Gender in Media*, n.d. www.seejane.org.

WEBSITES

About Face
www.about-face.org

About Face is a nonprofit that teaches girls how to assess media critically and highlights examples of media that objectify women.

Common Sense Media
www.commonsensemedia.org

Common Sense Media is an organization that educates children and their parents about media and includes ratings from kids and parents about TV shows and movies.

Geena Davis Institute on Gender in Media
www.seejane.org

The Geena Davis Institute on Gender in Media educates people about the importance of seeking gender balance, challenging stereotypes, and creating role models in media for children.

Women's Media Center
www.womensmediacenter.com

The Women's Media Center conducts research about women in media, works to raise awareness, and encourages strong and accurate media representation of women and girls.

INDEX

IMAGE **CREDITS**

ABOUT THE AUTHOR

Christine Evans is a freelance author living in Northern California with her husband and young daughters. Evans loves to write everything from picture books to magazine articles to books about women. When she's not writing or reading she loves to watch movies with her kids that feature awesome characters like Wonder Woman or Moana.